Tragedies and Trials are God's Perfect Work:

Tragedies and Trials are God's Perfect Work:

Geraldine Washington

Roaming Buffalo Publishing
2020

First Printing: 2020

ISBN 978-1-71674-739-7

Roaming Buffalo Publishing
Seattle, WA 98144

Dedication

I know the Holy Spirit's desire is for me to share with others this tragedy and the events surrounding it that led to my spiritual awakening. The goal of sharing my story is to show the glory of God. I can do nothing apart from God. So I dedicate this book to the sovereign will of God.

Second, I would like to dedicate this book to my parents, who sacrificed for their children and their grandchildren. My mother would always pray for her children and her children's children and those yet to be born. Her sense of God's eternal plan working through her family throughout time continues to guide me today.

Contents

Acknowledgements

My son Jack blessed me with the book, *This Year You Write Your Novel,* by Walter Mosley. I don't think I would have started or completed this task without the support, prayers, and encouragement of Jack and my daughter Pamela each step of the way. They worked closely with me; they edited and gave me ideas and scripture references. I would like to thank them for their help.

I would like to praise God and thank Him for Angela Bishop, Sarah Carleton (Red Adept Editing), and Jessica (Red Adept Editing), who edited this project along with my children.

I am also thankful to my brothers and sisters for their support and prayers.

Foreword

Loss can be a traumatic thing, especially if you have lost a loved one. Losing a home in a fire or the breakup of a marriage can be devastating. However, homes can be rebuilt, and marriages can be restored, but the deaths of two children and a husband are permanent and irreversible. How can anyone handle such catastrophic losses? Our Lord God brings us through more than we can imagine. This book you are about to read may bring tears to your eyes, especially if you have lost someone, but it will also allow you to see the sovereignty of our Lord Jesus Christ.

I read this book twice. The first time I read it, I cried for the author when she said she could not cry. This book tore my heart into many pieces. The second time I read the book, I saw the author's strength and the overwhelming love of God that brought her through her traumatic journey.

I see an author who writes from the heart. I see a mother who expresses her grief and her pain and, more importantly, her understanding of who God is and how He protects the hearts of His children. I see a daughter who knows that God knew how she would respond and the souls that she would touch through this experience. I see a human being who walked through a difficult journey and experienced the greatness of His power and His unconditional love. How can I say I see all these things in this author? I see these things because she is my sister.

She was a friend who liked reading and took me to the library with her. While she studied for exams, I would read and check out books to take home. She was a companion for me during the summer when we played games like red light green light. She was a diligent student who stayed up late studying for nursing exams and got up at one or two in the morning to continue to study. She was a compassionate person who showed how much she cared for others through her nursing career. She is not only an author who wants to share the love of God and His ability to walk with you through your journey, whatever it may be, but she is also my sister, who has shared every detail of her pain in order to encourage you and to give glory and honor to our God, knowing she would have never made it through this journey without Him.

As you read this book, may you receive God's unending love and grace that will carry you through your pain.

-Cheryl A. Noel, RN

April 2018

Introduction

In this book, my focus is on our sovereign God. God is love. He is abounding in mercy and grace. As immense as that sounds, God's whole being is so much larger. His attributes are many and awesome. I will focus on His awesome love because this is who He is. God's mercy and grace tie in closely with His love. I will share with you how our God's sovereignty operated in my life before, during, and many years after a tragic event in my personal life. My prayer is that by the strength of the Holy Spirit, all my words will be anointed. As I share my testimony, I pray that I may bring glory to God. I trust that these words will encourage each reader to hasten the pace of his or her spiritual walk and will desire to know more deeply our sovereign God and the Holy Spirit. I pray that you will focus on God's face, where you will find His love, mercy, and grace. I also pray that when you look at His hands, you will see the preeminent power of His grace and love working in all our circumstances. You will quickly know that God's guiding hand exists when there is joy, happiness, or peace, but you should also understand the same is true when there is disappointment, pain, or tragedy.*

*Note that all scripture references are taken from the New King James Version of the Bible.

My Life's Journey

There are many roads as we travel through life. Our cultures, family circumstances, abilities, heart's desires and, in many cases, financial statuses guide us through our lives. God's word will direct our lives only to the degree we believe in and trust Him as our Savior and Lord. I believe His will and care for us are sovereign. His love, mercy, grace, and forgiveness are the embodiment of His sovereignty.

I was born into a large Christian family of eight—four boys and four girls. I had two older sisters, three younger brothers, and a younger sister. I am a fraternal twin born fifteen minutes after my brother, making me the fourth child. My oldest sister is now with Jesus.

Our mother's example of faith and prayer in her life played a large part in shaping our values and beliefs. She would teach us how to live by sharing her sayings and expecting us to live by them. The two I remember best were: "On time, all the time, a little ahead of time is the best of time" and "Be the labor great or small, do it well or not at all." In addition to these sayings, she would post scriptures on the walls. I later learned that this was similar to customs in Jewish households. In these homes, the laws of God are above the entryways. When giving directions concerning the laws and commands, Moses told the Israelites to "write them on the doorpost of your house and on your gates" (Deuteronomy 6:9). These small things in our faith traditions across time enable us to see God's guiding hand. God's deepest desire is that each one of us be aware of His guiding hand in our lives.

Growing up in my Family

As is true in many families, we had our share of dysfunction in our home, but God's grace and our prayers promoted growth and change. Our father's support and mother's love and values created a secure, loving environment for us to mature in. As siblings, we were always very close, loving, and supportive of each other. When we were children, I would make mud pies, and my brothers would pretend to eat them. There were always games and fun with other children in the neighborhood. My mother's goal was for each one of her children to have a college education. The plan for us was college, marriage, and children. We started on that plan with the help of God and each other. We grew and started families of our own.

Mother

Our mother's primary activities were those of caring for a large family. She worked outside of the home but still made time to be active in her church. As children, we observed her reading the Bible and praying often. Although she loved her family greatly, she would never express her love verbally. She grew up during the Great Depression in a family in which people did not voice their feelings out loud. Her faith in Christ gave her the freedom to examine her life and expand her boundaries. In her later years, she learned to say, "I love you." Before she passed away, she would not end a conversation without telling her family members that she loved them. She also expected it from her family. One day, as I left for work, I overheard her tell her caregiver that I had forgotten to say, "I love you," so I turned back, kissed her, and told her I loved her.

My mother taught me the importance of prayer and Bible reading for young children. Her sayings were not always from scripture but were always words of wisdom that would direct a person to a life of value, honor, respect, and success. Her life was a sacrificial one. She worked many jobs to ensure that each one of her children got a college education. She was willing to give to others and make sacrifices, especially for her children. Her example enabled us, as brothers and sisters, to stand together and care for, support, and protect one another.

My mother had an extraordinary love and joy for each one of her children and grandchildren. She found joy in the accomplishments of all of us. She was patient with our little mistakes. My daughter shared with me the following story. One Christmas, she, her brother Jack, and their cousin Michelle were helping their grandmother make Christmas cakes. Their grandmother instructed and directed them in what they needed to do. When my mother was confident they understood, she went to the dining room to complete other tasks. They finished the cakes, and they all looked beautiful. Clowning around with Jack, my daughter lost her footing, fell, and sat on one of the cakes. Just at that moment, their grandmother returned and saw the cake on the seat of Pamela's pants! Her first response was a long laugh because of the hilarity of the situation.

Jack and Michelle joined their grandmother in her laughter. My mother did not rebuke her grandchildren or frown. She smiled and repaired the cake. That Christmas, everyone joked, "This is the cake Pamela sat on."

My mother was always there to pray for us, to support us, and to walk with us through every trial or problem. She prayed for her children, grandchildren, and those yet to be born. The value of unity and love in a family was important to her, and she passed that on to her children. Her example and standards would be my guide as I focused on my children's spiritual growth and care.

Father

My father loved each one of his grandchildren. He would smile serenely during their rough play and the general din of family gatherings. When he was younger, my father was a strict disciplinarian. He mellowed in his later years because of his pride in his children and his love for his grandchildren. A partial explanation of his uncanny serenity might be hearing loss, which was the result of working on the railroad near loud trains most of his career. When he finally received hearing aids, he would not wear them when all the grandchildren were around, because of the noise level.

Because my father was unable to hear clearly, he called one of his granddaughters Clara, even though her name was Zahra. To this day, she will smile her beautiful smile as she fondly remembers her grandfather who called her Clara.

My son Jack said that every time his shoes were untied, my father would bend over and tie them. Not long before my father's death, he said, "Jack, I will not always be here to tie your shoes."

Each grandchild has different fond memories of their grandfather, such as the fragrance of apple-scented tobacco wafting from his pipe, the aroma of his cigars, his special knock at the door, and his willingness to sew on a grandchild's loose button.

Jack told me that one Christmas, when most of the family was gathered together to celebrate the birth of Christ, his grandfather remarked, smiling, with tears in his eyes, "This might be the last time I will see so many of us gathered in one place." Everyone remembers him kneeling at his bedside in prayer.

Coming of Age

In the sixties, because of societal expectations and my insecurities, I felt I had two career options: nursing or teaching. I chose to become a nurse for two reasons. First, I knew that good communication—a gift I lacked—would be vital in the educational field. I was shy and introverted when I was young and learning to talk. There is a family story that as a child, my twin brother would speak for me whenever I needed something. I had an aunt who was a nurse, and she was a role model for that career. My father reminded me that I was squeamish and might vomit along with my patients, and I did have some gagging as a student nurse when one of my patients vomited in the beginning of my training, but I still became a nurse.

My four years of school in the College of Nursing were challenging. My father was proud and supportive. He requested prayer from his church during those difficult times. I later told him that it was those prayers that enabled me to graduate. I graduated in 1967 with a BS in nursing.

After I entered my career in nursing, I found joy, which assured me that despite my insecurities and the fact that limited choices appeared to direct me to become a nurse, my career was the sovereign will of God.

I first worked with pediatric patients, who were a great blessing because of my love for children. Later in my career, I would work with alcohol- and drug-abuse patients, for whom I faithfully made intercessory prayers.

Starting my own Family

I met my husband, Carroll, under an oak tree in front of the chemistry building on the campus of the University of Southwestern Louisiana. Most of our activities centered on the university. We were both Methodists and spent a lot of time at the Methodist student center. My husband assisted a close friend and me with a nursing project by getting materials needed and helping with the blueprint and design. Without his help, we would not have been successful. This close friend later became my bridesmaid.

After marriage, God blessed us with four beautiful children: a daughter, Pamela Lené, and three sons—Carroll Jack, Kevin Michael, and Octave David. After the birth of our fourth child, my husband thought that our family was complete, but I was a little unsure.

To limit our family size, we decided to have a bilateral tubal ligation. This procedure permanently prevents a woman from having any future pregnancies. As I said earlier, we make life decisions based on various factors. I chose to use God's word to find what direction to take in this area. I sincerely searched the Bible for guidance. However, in my spiritual blindness, I decided that I could not find anything that told me not to do it. I decided to have the procedure done. I was blind to God's full truth at that time.

I would come to know that God's words were plain and clear in this area. Genesis 1:28 states, "Then God blessed them, and God said to them, 'Be fruitful and multiply; fill the earth and subdue it...'" In Psalm 127:3–5, Solomon says, "Behold, children are a heritage from the Lord, the fruit of the womb is a reward. Like arrows in the hand of a warrior, so are the children of one's youth. Happy is the man who has his quiver full of them...." Later, I realized that my decision was not God's perfect will.

Nevertheless, in spite of our mistakes, God is sovereign, and His love, grace, mercy, and forgiveness are always present. God's word gives us ample assurance of His mercy and grace even when our direction is misguided. Paul, in Romans 8:28, says, "And we know that all things work together for good to those who love God, to those who are called according to His purpose." I decided to focus on my four children's spiritual growth and care. They were gifts and rewards from God. My mother would be my example.

Kevin

Kevin Michael was born August 19, 1972, and was our third child, two years younger than his brother Carroll Jack, who was two years younger than Pamela. He started talking much later than most children. This speech delay caused a little concern for his father and me, but in other ways, his development was normal. In fact, Kevin was a very bright child. When he started talking, he spoke clearly in complete sentences. There was never any baby talk for Kevin. I think he listened and learned to communicate when he felt he needed to talk.

When Kevin was four and a half years old, his younger brother, Octave, was born. There were signs of jealousy at first, but I worked with Kevin, helping him to understand that he was loved. I explained to him that his baby brother needed a big brother to love him and to take care of him. With constant support, love, and direction, Kevin finally grew to adore his baby brother Octave.

Kevin's hair was coarse and curly, and sometimes combing it before school was a difficult job that would result in crying and tears. I later decided that combing his hair every morning was not so important. I thought that maybe just a "brush" would do. His father had God's grace to take on this responsibility.

He loved participating in prayer time and Bible stories with his sister and brothers. I had to coax him to pray because he felt awkward praying out loud. He would give me the special secretive smile and bright eyes that meant, "I have a secret that I'm not yet ready to share." He would always obey and pray. Our family prayer time was a particular moment of joy for me. It was a blessing to see Kevin's expression. He would take his turn saying a short prayer. He enjoyed discussing and reading Bible stories with the siblings.

When Kevin got off the school bus, he was sometimes very loud. He made friends quickly and enjoyed them. He never showed shyness when he was playing or having fun with his buddies, although sometimes he was shy with strangers. He had a special relationship with his older brother. His older brother, Jack, was a Cub Scout. Kevin looked forward to being old enough to become a Cub Scout and spoke of it frequently.

I enjoyed their closeness, which was what family is all about. It was a great blessing to witness the joy, unity, and love in our family, values I'd seen in my family as a child.

Kevin was close to his father. As my husband, Carroll, watched TV, Kevin would sit on the floor at his feet. Carroll noticed Kevin's interest in soccer and bought him a soccer ball. The ball was one of the things they bonded over.

Athletically gifted, Kevin enjoyed playing soccer and participating in gymnastics. He showed great pride in his success and was very skillful. I finally understood my mother's joy at her children's accomplishments. I experienced this at every gymnastics performance I attended. There would be more accomplishments as time ushered in maturity, growth, and skills.

Watching Kevin ride his bicycle unsteadily alongside the curb with his older brother made me uneasy. I knew he would improve in time. This activity was great fun for both of them and part of the growth process. They spent many long hours playing and having fun with each other. There were broken light fixtures and busted lips when their excitement while indoors took them into play that was more appropriate for outdoors. They were friends as well as brothers and loved and enjoyed each other.

Our neighborhood was a new development when we built our home. There were many construction sites and wooded areas in which Jack and Kevin played and explored. They would spend hours romping, investigating, and just having fun until a worker or homeowner would sternly remind them that housing development sites were not always safe. To the boys, the pleasure and joy of being together and sharing were worth being scolded by the construction workers.

When they walked to school, they would sing rap music, which was fun for both of them. When Jack shared this with me, it brought me joy and laughter. I usually drove them to school and would announce "Next stop!" for whichever school was my first drop-off site. After that child got out of the car, I would say "All aboard!" for the next school. These moments created memories that sustained our family in the future by helping us to form a close bond with each other.

There were many times we went out to eat as a family. The children's favorite restaurant was Mr. Gatti's Pizza. Eating out was exciting for the entire family, one of those activities that we've remembered all our lives. These were beautiful moments of laughter and fun.

Boys are usually close to their mothers in unique ways. Kevin, in particular, communicated with me through his smiles and his expressive eyes even before he spoke. As he grew, he would share his concerns as he adjusted to being a big brother. He would allow me to comfort him and guide him in a way that mothers often do with their sons.

As Kevin grew, we would have small family birthday celebrations. Kevin had a fantastic formal birthday party with friends and family when he turned seven. I will always remember his special smile and bright eyes that day. It was an enjoyable time for everyone—Jack, Pamela, Octave, and other family members. With joyful anticipation, I looked forward to my children's birthdays, which were marked by milestones in their growth and skills. The years passed by much too quickly.

Octave

Octave David was born on March 16, 1977. He was named Octave in honor of a favorite uncle. We used "David" as a middle name in case "Octave" seemed too old-fashioned. He was lovingly called Tave.

When he should have been going through the terrible twos, he instead had a quiet and sweet personality. Seldom did he cry, and never did he have a temper tantrum. The few times I remember him crying were when I would leave for work. His tears were brief because his sister comforted him. He loved Pamela as much as she adored him. He had a white blanket that he carried around all the time just like the *Peanuts* character Linus. He held this blanket tightly with one hand, the end of it near his lower lip. Everyone called it his *blank-let*.

I felt joy in teaching Tave how to say his blessing before each meal—the same blessing his older brothers and sister had learned: "God is great. God is good. Let us thank Him for our food. Amen." Tave would only say, "Bless the eggs" for breakfast, or "Bless the chicken" for dinner. The main dish or his favorite food was blessed. I needed to remember that a child of almost three had a significant amount of growth potential in the area of vocabulary.

I worked the night shift, which allowed me to spend time with my children and bring them to and from school. Tave would spend time with his great-grandmother during the day so that I could get much-needed sleep. When Tave returned home after spending time with his great-grandmother, there was an excited cry of, "Mama, there is Daddy!" as his father's car came into view. To the almost three-year-old boy, Daddy was big and strong and important in his life. Tave would squeal with laughter as Daddy threw him into the air and caught him. He would spend hours on Daddy's lap. Those were hard but fun times.

We had plans for Tave's future. We'd get him a backyard swing set. Carroll believed that Tave would excel in school when the time came. He was proud of Tave and loved him very much.

Tave enjoyed Bible stories. Pointing to the Bible I used frequently, he would say, "Mama, look—Jesus." This Bible had a bright-colored cover with a picture of Jesus sitting with a child held in His arms and with other children sitting at His feet.

Tave also shared prayer time and Bible stories every night. Though he was not old enough to take his turn praying, he quietly listened to his older brothers and sister. Every night, we said the Lord's Prayer together as a family. Tave would say it with us or just listen and learn from his older brothers and sister. Next, we recited together, "Now I lay me down to sleep. I pray the Lord, my soul to keep..." To see him grow and learn in this area was wonderful. These were the basics of prayer. As the children got older, I taught them the importance and purpose of talking to God. I tried to teach them that it was the way to develop a relationship with the living God. Prayer was a spiritual weapon against everything that opposed God. We were the temples of the Holy Spirit, who dwells in each one of us.

Sunday morning meant Sunday school. There was a big stained-glass window in front of the church we attended. This window had a picture of Jesus kneeling in prayer. When we arrived at the church, there would be wide-eyed excitement from Tave at seeing another image of Jesus. With the same gestures and pointed finger, Tave

This picture was drawn by Tave's niece Teresa Blakeslee.

would announce, "Mama, look—Jesus!" Jesus had indeed become a friend to Tave.

Jack had spent months helping Tave with toilet training. This time together worked well in two ways. First, it resulted in a good relationship between Jack and Tave. Jack would sit by the toilet and throw wet toilet paper against the wall to amuse his little brother as he tried to use the commode. Octave would laugh every time the paper would stick to the wall. A great camaraderie developed between them. Second, when Tave was toilet-trained and ready for training pants, he experienced a significant change. He was no longer my baby but a big boy. Those changes gave me feelings of both pride and loss. I knew that Tave would be my last baby. I thought how God placed the desire in every mother's heart to hold a child in her arms and to love and nourish that child. I realized then that I might have taken the wrong direction. But I knew with all my heart that God's mercy, love, and grace would always be there. I had to trust and have faith in my sovereign God.

Tave was still my special baby whom I loved very much. I was proud of his accomplishments. He was a big boy and was toilet-trained, but I would continue to hold him tightly and love him and watch him grow up.

Friday, February 15, 1980

The time lapse between actual events and my testimony is the result of God's providence. His ways are not our ways.

It was a full and beautiful day on Friday the 15th, 1980, sandwiched between Valentine's Day and my twelfth wedding anniversary. My father-in-law had sent me a large box of chocolate candy. My husband and I were planning to eat out for our anniversary two days later if I was able to take a day off work. I was still working as a supervisor at a local hospital. On Friday, I had scheduled an appointment to get my hair done as I did every week. The older children were at school, and Tave would be going with me. He was almost three. His birthday was March 16, only a month away.

Every morning, I now pray the following prayer: "Lord, I don't know what the day holds, but You do. I don't know what's in it for You or me, but I'm Yours. I invite you to guide me one step at a time. I want Your power to mark my steps. Stop me if I'm moving in the wrong direction. Push me if I'm sluggish. Get me going again if I'm hesitant. Correct my course if I get out of line. But don't let me go my own way. Fill me with Your presence and power." The Holy Spirit led me to this prayer about six years ago. I don't remember the author or source of this prayer. Unfortunately, I did not say this prayer on that morning.

Tave and I drove to the beautician in time for my scheduled appointment. My son was wearing his first pair of training pants. As we arrived at the beauty shop, I introduced him to the ladies present. I then placed him in a chair, where he sat quietly while I had my hair washed and set. The other children in the shop ran around, pulling magazines out of racks, and one even knocked over a plant. In contrast, I was complimented on how well Tave behaved and how cute he was. His praiseworthy behavior was partly the result of his shyness around strangers. Nevertheless, I felt the happiness of being blessed with a unique and adorable child. I was experiencing the joy my mother always had for each one of her children.

When we left the shop, I held him close as we walked to the car. As I held him, I realized his pants were wet and was jerked back to the present. I had neglected to ask him if he needed to use the toilet for the last two hours. I held him tighter and smiled. His accident was due to my carelessness, and it was his first day wearing training pants. The time would come when wet pants would be a thing of the past.

After the hairdresser, we stopped at my grandmother's house—she lived nearby—and I changed Tave into dry pants so that he would be comfortable. We had a good visit with her. She would care for Tave while I was working. She had a close relationship with him, and we had an enjoyable stay. We next went to his cousin Brian's nursery school to give him a ride home. Brian was one year younger than Tave. We were planning to place Tave in nursery school soon. Later that afternoon, when the older children got out of school for the week, I was scheduled to bring Pamela to a dance class and Jack to a Cub Scout meeting. Kevin talked excitedly about his soccer game the next morning. I got his soccer uniform ready and laid it out. When it was time to drive Pamela and Jack to their activities, we all went together. I dropped Pamela off at her dance class first, and Jack went to his Scout meeting. Tave, Kevin, and I drove home. I would pick up Pamela and Jack later.

I vaguely remember doing some activities after arriving home. Just before it was time to get Pamela and Jack, I was at the dining room table with Tave, looking at his brightly colored Bible with the picture of Jesus on the cover. As Tave had done so many times before, he pointed to the Bible and the image of Jesus. This time, he said, "Mama, look—Jesus Christ." That was the first time he ever said, "Christ," when referring to Jesus. I would later understand why God allowed me to remember this so clearly. We then got in the car and drove to pick up Pamela and Jack. I have only three other memories of that day. After I picked Pam up from dance class, I remember deciding not to stop at the library to drop off books that needed to be returned. Instead, I went down a street that was not as busy and congested.

At first, I had no memories of what happened after I had turned down that street and the two weeks that followed. When my memories began to return, they were vague and confusing. It was like awakening from a dream and not knowing that I had awakened at all. I would pray that I was still dreaming so I would not have to face what had happened.

The Accident

The next memory I have is riding in a wheelchair on March 2. I did not ask any questions about where I was or what had happened.

When I got home, I walked into Tave and Kevin's room. I saw my husband and asked him, "Where are Tave and Kevin?"

He replied, "Don't you remember, Geraldine? You were in an accident, and Tave and Kevin died."

I could not respond. His words did not register at all. I showed no emotion. I shed no tears. I believe that God had me in a spiritual cocoon of His love, mercy, and grace from minutes before the accident until I was discharged from the hospital and even later. I had amnesia, and God only removed it gradually when He allowed me to start having some memories of this painful time. In His sovereignty, He was slowly leading me back to reality out of my cocoon.

Psalm 91:11–12 says, "For He shall give His angels charge over you, to keep you in all your ways. In their hands, they shall bear you up, lest you dash your foot against a stone." Is this not our sovereign God, a God of awesome love, mercy, grace, and wisdom? God in His sovereignty knew that I was not ready physically or emotionally to face the full extent of this tragedy.

My next memory is of my husband taking me to Tave and Kevin's gravesite. Once again, I did not cry or show any real emotion. I only bent over and picked up dirt at the grave. I did let my husband know that I was glad they were next to their grandfather, my husband's father. My husband shared with me later how difficult that was for him. He was hurting deeply over the death of our two sons; he was feeling guilt and fear. He did not understand my lack of emotions and tears. He made every effort to comfort his two living children, and in doing so, he found they would be the ones to comfort him. Other family members did not understand. I was not aware and could not know at that time, though I would find out later. I was still wrapped in the spiritual cocoon of God's love, mercy, and grace.

As time passed, I became more aware of my surroundings and started to ask questions. I would know later that I was still in God's cocoon, but He had opened it a little wider. God's gift of amnesia continued to protect me during this traumatic time. I learned that my brothers and sisters had been around me with their love, prayers, and support from the time of the accident. I gathered details about the crash from each of my brothers and sisters as well as my mother, Carroll, and Pamela. I also obtained my medical records. In the process of gathering details, I was able to understand more clearly. I comprehended God's sovereignty, awesome love, mercy, and grace at a more profound depth.

Pamela told me that at the time of the accident that she'd been lying across the back seat, reading (this being before seat belt laws). She said many times after the crash, "Mama, you stopped." I did not remember this until years later when I started to understand what had happened. Pamela said, "I tried to wake you after the accident." She told me that I'd been lying over Tave and Kevin as though I wanted to protect them. Pamela said, "I was not able to wake you."

Pamela had emotional scars because of this traumatic experience. We talked about it many times over the years. Our preeminent God over time provided the needed love, mercy, and grace to heal and restore Pamela. The only physical injury she had was a bruised eye.

In the confusion, Pamela had been left behind by the ambulance. This incident was tragic, but God in His sovereignty did not forget Jack, who would learn that his two brothers had died in the accident while he was at his Cub Scout meeting. Pamela was able to call my youngest brother, Leslie, who is now a pastor, for a ride from the accident site. When he arrived, she directed him to get Jack from his meeting. At that time, Pamela was eleven years old, and Jack was nine.

The ambulance had taken Tave and me to Lafayette Charity Hospital. Kevin went to Lafayette General Hospital because his condition appeared more critical and the neurological services were better at that facility. My older sister, Pearl, arrived quickly and, after seeing my condition, had me transferred to Lafayette General Hospital. Our preeminent God was there at every step with His love, grace, and wisdom. I was told Tave died on a stretcher next to me in the emergency room at Charity Hospital.

Leslie went to Lafayette General Hospital to check on Kevin. When he arrived at the hospital, a doctor told him that Kevin had died. I know that this sudden and tragic news was devastating to my family. It was especially difficult for my father, who had a close relationship with Kevin and Octave. God did not allow me to face the full weight of this tragedy. It would have been like a powerful locomotive coming toward me at tremendous speed with me frozen in its path.

The Hospital Stay

At Lafayette General Hospital, the doctors told my family there was a possibility that I might not live. I was diagnosed with a closed head injury, right periorbital fracture, and multiple lacerations. The doctors saw the amnesia as being typical of a closed head injury. My condition was critical, according to the medical records. I know that I had spiritual amnesia, which was the result of God placing me in the sovereign protective cocoon of His love, mercy, and grace. My parents, husband, brothers, sisters, family, and friends prayed to God for a miraculous healing.

According to my medical records, I was in the hospital for two weeks. My mother told me that I had severe pain in my head and neck. The medical staff frequently gave me medication. God was sheltering me. Medically, this degree of pain was common after a closed head injury and right orbital fractures. Forty years later, an MRI revealed that I had chronic focal encephalomalacia – a usually debilitating condition resulting from the oxygen deprivation of the brain for a time. The symptoms include diminished motor skills, visual impairment, memory loss, and mood swings.

I was lethargic and sluggish and did not always respond to my brothers or appear to recognize them. My younger brothers, Chris and Alfred, told me that they asked me to squeeze their hands if I understood what was said or if I remembered them. Sometimes I would respond to their requests, and other times I would not. I did not speak much during that time. The doctors were very concerned about my lack of communication, especially because I did not ask about my daughter, Pamela. In my medical records, the doctors noted, "She has not expressed interest in seeing her daughter, even when questioned." I think my mother helped to ease their concerns by telling them that it was normal because "I was a quiet person."

The doctors encouraged my family to let me know about the deaths of my two youngest sons. Later, I checked with every family member and discovered that no one had told me about their deaths. My youngest sister, Cheryl, said that I appeared to be too weak and confused at that time. God would not allow His protective cocoon of love to be disturbed until it was His sovereign will.

When I communicated at all during the two-week hospital stay, it was through my spirit. We are composed of a body and spirit made in the image and likeness of God. John 4:24 states, "God is Spirit, and those who worship Him must worship in spirit and truth."

###

Genesis 1:26 states, "Then God said, 'Let Us make man in Our image, according to Our likeness.'" The Godhead or Holy Trinity includes the Father, the Son, and the Holy Spirit. In Deuteronomy 6:4, God says to Israel, "Hear, O Israel: The Lord our God, the Lord is one!"

In John 14:10, Jesus says, "Do you not believe that I am in the Father and the Father in Me? The words that I speak to you, I do not speak on My own authority, but the Father who dwells in Me does the works." Concerning the Third Person of the Holy Trinity, in the book of Luke, chapter 4:18, Jesus says, "The Spirit of the Lord is upon Me, Because He has anointed Me to preach the gospel to the poor..." Paul says, in I Thessalonians 5:23, "Now may the God of peace Himself sanctify you completely; and may your whole spirit, soul, and body be preserved blameless at the coming of our Lord Jesus Christ."

A human person consists of both body and soul. Without the body, we cannot communicate with the people around us in the physical world. We can, however, connect to the spiritual world with our spirit or soul. God was in control of my whole being during this time. While my body was damaged, I could still talk to the living God and He with me.

My family shared with me things I said during those two weeks that caused me to be in awe and wonder at the wisdom, love, and care of God. As Psalm 113:5 states, "Who is like the Lord our God, Who dwells on high."

I had vague memories for a while afterward, but I had spiritual amnesia. Medically, I was not oriented to a person, time, or place. My brother Chris told me that I said, "The angels of God are rubbing the memory from my mind."

According to my medical records, the doctors' next decision was a psychiatric consult. When the doctors asked my husband and me about this, my husband told me I said, "I don't need a psychiatrist." He agreed with me, and they did not do a consult. I later would know it was my husband and the Spirit of God who made that decision.

There is a note by the physician in my records: "Patient and husband have decided that a psychiatric consult is unnecessary and do not wish to have one, will hold off at present." I know that God did not want a psychiatric doctor to interfere with the work He was doing. I was secure in the loving arms of God.

As I was interviewing my siblings for this book, Cheryl shared something extraordinary with me about my hospital stay. She stayed with me to help with my care. As she was combing my hair, my eyes were closed, and she knew for sure that I was talking to God. She heard me say two words:

"Tave too." Because she lived in Arizona, Cheryl did not realize that we called the baby Tave instead of Octave. Even as I write this book, I become aware of God's movement during one of the darkest times of my life and am able to comprehend his love for me. I believe that I was in a conversation with God and He said to me that He had taken Tave as well as Kevin.

I have prayed and asked God to enable me to remember. He did not answer that prayer. However, God is sovereign, and our part is to trust and rest in Him. Proverbs 3:5 states, "Trust in the Lord with all your heart, and lean not on your own understanding."

The doctors in their discharge notes wrote, "She has been a little lethargic, but in the last couple of days she has been more aware of her surroundings and appears to be aware of the tragic situation of the death of her two youngest children." There were no notes in the medical records saying that the doctors told me about the deaths of my sons. I know my family did not tell me. I don't understand why the doctors made this assessment, but I suspect that the Spirit of God said something through me that led them to believe that I knew my sons had died. The Spirit of our sovereign God told me about the deaths of my sons. Our awesome God, who is mercy and grace, filled me with a love we can't imagine.

In the book of Psalms, you will find many scriptures praising His greatness. Psalm 145:3 states, "Great is the Lord, and greatly to be praised; and His greatness is unsearchable." My spirit was aware of the death of my sons.

###

On March 2, I was discharged. As I said earlier, my first memory was of my mother pushing me in a wheelchair. But I was still very much in God's spiritual and emotional cocoon, wrapped in His love and grace.

According to my family, the doctors and nursing staff gave me excellent care during my two-week hospital stay. They have my thanks, and I praise God for them.

The Funeral

The funeral was on February 21. It was the sixth day of my hospitalization. The service was at the same church where Tave had so many times before pointed to the kneeling Jesus on the stained glass window and said, "Mama, look—Jesus."

God had given me a clear memory from right before the accident. This most precious memory will last a lifetime and be a blessing over and over again. When Tave pointed to the Bible and said, "Mama, look—Jesus Christ," I was not aware of what a remarkable blessing it would be. Did he somehow know he would soon be going to meet his friend Jesus?

I think at that moment he saw and knew Jesus as the Christ, the long-awaited king and savior. In the same way, Matthew 16:16 gives Peter's great confession: "You are the Christ, the Son of the living God."

Pearl shared with me an example of God's sovereignty and protective love from the funeral. A relative took pictures of my sons in their coffins but was unable to develop the film. Someone else attempted to record the funeral service but was also unsuccessful. God's plan was for me not to have a permanent record of the funeral. God was continuing to protect me. Pearl told me small details about the funeral and the children's choir that performed at the funeral.

Pamela and Jack did not attend the funeral. I believe that this was God's providence and loving will. Jack later told me that he wished he could have gone to the funeral to hold his father's hand. Pearl said that my twin brother, Gerald, grieved for my two sons at the funeral and burial. He felt weak at the funeral and had to stay at our mother's home for a few days before being able to go back to his home in Houston. Gerald and I are emotionally tied together from our time in the womb, but I really can't explain the bond. I believe he was carrying my grief when I was unable.

Our preeminent God is the only one who understands. The depths of His mysterious wonders are beyond our discovery. In Romans 11:34, Paul asks, "For who has known the mind of the Lord?"

Separation

Over the next months, I remained in emotional amnesia by God's sovereign control. I don't think I went through any of the stages of grief. After the death of a child, the marriage sometimes falls apart because both the husband and wife are hurting deeply and neither can comfort the other. The impact of the tragedy was starting to dawn on me at that time, but I was still secure in His love. Our loving God provided comfort and love to my husband as He did for me, but I don't know how much Carroll was willing to receive it. My husband's father had been struck dead by lightning when Carroll was only eight years old. I later learned that my husband was angry at God because of that. The death of our two sons just increased his questions, anger, and confusion about his relationship with God. My husband had used, on occasion, marijuana recreationally. After the accident, my husband began to self-medicate with illegal drugs. The death of our children and his newfound addiction contributed to our separation.

In August, six months after the deaths of my sons, Cheryl invited me to visit her in Arizona. My husband and I were still separated. The day before I left to visit Cheryl, I knelt and prayed for God to bless me with a more understanding husband and a set of twins. I think I made this request because I'm a twin. The twins would be a boy and girl. The boy's name would be Michael David, and the girl's name would be Angel Teresa. Michael and David were the middle names of Kevin and Tave. I was asking God for a miracle. I'd had the procedure that prevented me from having more children. I was calling on my God of mercy and grace, knowing that He was more than able to help. He was a faithful and loving father. I was beginning to be in touch with reality. I was more aware of my circumstances, and I was giving voice to my soul's desires. God was bringing me to a deeper level of healing and restoration.

During that time of prayer, I heard God's voice telling me to pray for Carroll. Though He had spoken to me during my hospital stay as He made me aware of Tave and Kevin's death, this was the first time I heard and remembered what He said. I was obedient and prayed for Carroll as God directed.

Baptism in the Holy Spirit

The trip to visit Cheryl in Arizona was a blessing and a refreshing change. It was an exciting trip for Pamela and Jack, who were able to see many new sights, learn more about the world, and enjoy family. It was a break for them from the tragedy and uncertainty that were now always present in their lives.

It was a special time to share with Cheryl spiritually. We loved each other very much, and she gave me a lot of significant emotional support. The continual presence of my sovereign, loving God was working in my life. Visiting Cheryl would provide the tools needed to bring me complete healing and restoration.

I attended Cheryl's church, Landmark Bible Church, where I received the baptism of the Holy Spirit with the gift of tongues. The Holy Spirit language is an essential part of my devotional life with the Lord. It enlarges worship, deepens prayer, and strengthens all areas of the spirit. When we speak in tongues, we can personally increase our spirit and build ourselves up in our most holy faith.

In 1 Corinthians 14:4, Paul says, "He who speaks in tongues edifies himself, but he who prophesies edifies the church." He also says, "I thank my God I speak with tongues more than you all." This gift is for God's glory and our edification.

God removed His spiritual cocoon and emotional amnesia and replaced it with the baptism of the Holy Spirit and its unique gift of tongues. This tool God used to initiate my total healing. God had many gifts to aid His children. For me, it was this special gift. I spent every quiet moment praying in tongues. I spent many nights and days praying in the spirit. The result was the edification and strengthening of my faith in the spirit. The Holy Spirit is real and relevant and able to turn each one of our days into something beautiful.

The same day that I received the baptism of the Holy Spirit, a prophet, Dr. Bill Hamon, gave me a prophecy of encouragement. It was a word of hope for the future and God's hand guiding my life:

> I see you like a new chick just hatched out of the egg. And I see the great mother hen, the Holy Spirit, just overshadowing you. And I see Jesus there just watching over you, protecting you. And the Lord says daughter, I'm not expecting a whole lot out of you. I'm not requiring much out of you. Just receive my food, and receive my blessings. And I'm going to protect you from the old hawks that try to come swooping down and harming you. And

you felt the pressure; you felt the persecution in some areas, some difficulties, some restriction. For the Lord says, "Daughter, just stay under my wings; stay under my love. My wings are my praise and prayer. My wings are my faithfulness and goodness. My wings are my word and my spirit. My wings are my love and my care. Stay under my love and my care. I don't want you to try to run around and win the whole world. I just want you to be a shining light and let my bright light shine through you." And the Lord says, "Those you're concerned about and that area that you're concerned about is all being worked by the angels of the Lord." And God says, "I'm going to work for you right now, and I'm going to make miracles take place in your life. And I'm going to work everything out. And then later, I'm going to teach you how to do it, and we'll work together," saith the Lord.

The prophecy was the voice of God, who is Love. The words I most needed to hear at that time were, "And the Lord says those you're concerned about and that area you're concerned about is all being worked on by the angels of the Lord." They were words of assurance and comfort. My concern at that time was my husband and our marriage. The rest of the prophecy was precious promises, blessings, and the hope of being used by my God for His glory.

When I returned home, I knew that the angels of the Lord had indeed worked on that which I was concerned about, as the prophecy had said. God did a great transformation in my husband's life, allowing him to deal with the addiction, pain, and anger he held toward God. This work was not complete in either my husband's or my life. There was still healing needed in our family, but God was faithful and would complete the work he'd begun. Paul tells us, in Philippians 1:6, that "being confident of this very thing, that He who has begun a good work in you will complete it until the day of Jesus Christ."

Healing

God restored the relationship between my husband and me over the years that followed. There would be healing, forgiveness, and grieving to work through as a family. My husband felt that his addiction was due in part to the death of our sons. Carroll had to come to a place where he realized he had a need only God could satisfy. In all circumstances where there is tragedy, loss, or death, God's grace is available to meet one's need. Through prayer, love, and support, my husband eventually reached out and received God's love and grace. The healing of our wounds would be a long road, but our God, who is full of grace and love, is more than able.

I knew that at this time the healing process had begun. I remember crying and feeling a painful void because of the death of my sons. Anytime I saw a two- or three-year-old child, my heart ached, and I felt empty. My boys' birthdays, as well as the anniversary of their deaths, were difficult. God's presence in my life as I prayed in tongues strengthened me when I grieved.

There were many times I asked God, "Why both of them?" I don't know if the pain would have been any less if only one of my sons had died. I asked many times the simple question, "Why?" Our sovereign God, even in His silence, will always answer our questions. While it may not be the answer we want or expect, it may be that He is filling us with peace and assurance of His love, mercy, and grace. The answer may just be the awareness that He will be with us, walking by our side or even carrying us.

Pamela and Jack later shared with me the pain, fear, and uncertainty they felt during my hospitalization. No one talked to them. The adults talked around them, making them more concerned and full of questions. Each person was hurting deeply and dealing with his or her pain.

Jack said, "I did not remember that much. I may have been in shock." He remembered his father holding him and Pamela tightly and crying. My son said that having so many people come to our house was challenging and made him uneasy. My grandmother, who had looked after Tave, stayed with Carroll and the children while I was in the hospital. Jack's great-grandmother was a comfort to him during that time of confusion and uncertainty. He told me that while she was with them, he wanted to fly his kite, but the string that was full of knots. Jack still remembers his great-grandmother patiently taking out each knot so that he was able to fly his kite. He felt her peace and quietness of spirit. She had experienced the death of two young daughters. I know that at the time of my children's need, God placed a person who understood in their path. Jack's great-grandmother was able to let that same support and love flow through her that she received during her loss. My grandmother did this without words. She was able to comfort, bless, and give solace to Jack.

Love is a powerful thing as we journey through life. The only source of this kind of love comes from our sovereign, loving father, God, who is love, and His son Jesus Christ. Jack missed his brothers growing up. Kevin's absence left a void in his life. The passing of the years slowly brought him healing.

Pamela was concerned that I might not know her when I returned from the hospital because of conversations she had overheard about my amnesia. She was also worried about her father, remembering how he had held her and Jack tightly and how he had cried. She told me that she could see that he was in a lot of pain and wondered how she would take care of him if something happened to me. Many times, when she came home, Pamela was hoping Kevin and Tave would be there. I had the same desire and prayed for that to happen. In an effort to protect Pam and Jack from further trauma, our family decided that the children would skip the funeral. My surviving children now feel that attending the funeral might have provided closure.

I remember worrying about the possible deaths of Pamela and Jack too, but my husband assured me that God would not allow it. His words were encouraging and supportive. My husband began voicing increased faith and trust in God after we got back together. With the passing of time, we were able to share and support each other more. My husband shared the emptiness he felt without Kevin at his feet as he watched TV and the void left from Tave not being there.

There were times I heard the music from an ice cream truck coming down my street and remembered that I did not have the opportunity to take Tave by the hand and buy ice cream for him from this brightly colored vehicle. There were other times I looked in the backyard and recalled the swing set his father and I had planned to purchase. Sometimes I remembered Kevin's soccer ball he left behind, which I kept in a large basket in my living room. I did not know what to do or how to feel at those moments.

I now believe more deeply that God is Love. When there are tears at these times, I know God weeps with me. I can trust the Holy Spirit to hold me in His arms and comfort me and bring a unique and precious memory from the past. For example, at one time during a moment of grief, I remembered a time when I held Kevin and told him how much I loved him and how special he was. I was able to see and remember his beautiful-secretive smile. He was having some jealousy over his baby brother. The Holy Spirit gave me this clear memory, which gave me joy. We don't need to ask "Why?" constantly. We just need to trust His faithfulness and remember that God promises to work all things out together for good.

In addition to keeping me from remembering the day of the accident and my hospital stay, the head injury left me with damage to my short-term memory. To help with this issue, my husband suggested we attend a local university class that would give me tools to improve my short-term memory. I would need this when I returned to work. It was a difficult task in the beginning, but by the grace of God, these tools gave me success in improving my memory. God's grace was meeting me at my point of need as I placed my faith in Jesus Christ. When I returned to work, my coworkers gave me a welcome-back party. This party and the kindness of my colleagues were precious drops of blessing falling from heaven. They were yet another example of my sovereign God's love.

As the years passed, Jack and Pamela advanced in school. I became more acutely aware of Tave and Kevin's absence, and I found myself often wondering what they might have become. Even in this, our sovereign God's grace, mercy, and love were in abundance. I was proud of Jack and

Pamela's accomplishments. It appeared that God had given them a double portion; Pamela and Jack never had any of the problems you sometimes find in the teenage years. In spite of the death of their brothers, they were both excellent students through high school and college. Their success was the work of our sovereign God of mercy and grace. Psalm 103:17 says, "But the mercy of the Lord is from everlasting to everlasting on those who fear Him, And His righteousness to children's children."

In the book of Samuel, we see more of the compassion, grace, and love of our sovereign God. Hannah prayed in 1 Samuel 1:11, "O Lord of hosts, if You will indeed look on the affliction of Your maidservant and remember me, and not forget Your maidservant, but will give Your maidservant a male child, then I will give him to the Lord all the days of his life..." Later we read that God blessed Hannah with more children. "And the Lord visited Hannah so that she conceived and bore three sons and two daughters. Meanwhile, the child Samuel grew before the Lord" (1 Samuel 2:21). These passages in Samuel show us that God gives abundantly above all that we can comprehend. This is the nature of our sovereign God who is love.

The passage of time continued to bring changes that lessened the pain of the deaths of my children. God's grace was always there in abundance with more blessings as I kept my eyes focused on His loving face, trusting His heart of love when I could not see His hand.

Death of My Husband

My husband died in March 1990, ten years after the death of my sons, from a massive heart attack. He died after a beautiful family Christmas, one that we would always remember. The same was true of the Christmas before the death of Kevin and Tave. God blessed us with ten years of healing, spiritual growth, and restoration before taking my husband home. Our sovereign God is all knowing and abounds in love, grace, and wisdom.

We have to focus on God's loving face and His grace, not our circumstances. After my husband's death, God surrounded me with peace that surpasses all understanding. As Paul explains in Philippians 4:7, "... and the peace of God, which surpasses all understanding, will guard your hearts and minds through Jesus Christ." God continued to heal and restore me. The Holy Spirit's presence, power, and gifts were necessary at this time.

Deeper Healing

As the years passed, the Holy Spirit helped me to remember that my sons were not lost but were with Jesus. I watched my nieces and nephews who were close in age to Kevin and Tave, and the sight of them growing up was a poignant reminder of the death of my sons. After attending the graduation of a niece who was Tave's age, I went home and cried. During the continuing process of healing, God's love and grace were always there in abundance. As the years passed, the reminders became less painful. That understanding was an epiphany for me. I could suddenly see and understand their deaths in a new way. I came to a more profound place of knowledge.

The comfort and love I received from God in my pain and at the time of my need were able to flow through me. The Holy Spirit helped me to focus less on myself and more on others. I knew that God's plan for our lives was to mold us into the image of His son, Jesus. To be truly human, one needed to be like Jesus.

As my focus changed, the reminders became more of a blessing. To see my nieces and nephews growing, maturing, and succeeding was a joy to me. I used that time as an opportunity to pray for them. When I came to that stage in my healing, God could freely pour more blessings into my life.

Reading about Joseph in the book of Genesis helped me to see how God enables us to forget the past and look to the future. Joseph was sold into slavery by his brothers and taken to Egypt. There he was jailed after being unjustly accused of a crime. God was with Joseph and granted him the gift of interpretation of dreams. Joseph became ruler over Egypt second only to Pharaoh. Genesis 41:50–52 says that "And to Joseph were born two sons before the years of famine came... Joseph called the name of the firstborn Manasseh: 'For God has made me forget all my toil and all my father's house.' And the name of the second he called Ephraim: 'For God has caused me to be fruitful in the land of my affliction.'"

God helps us to restore our sense of well-being and build solid foundations for our future as he heals our past hurts. Much like a broken bone, the mended portion is often stronger than the original if it is given time to heal. The story of Joseph's life is an example of this. God helps us to not look back at pain, sorrow, and depression. He gives us faith instead of despair and sends us more blessings. God blessed Joseph with two sons. Joseph was fruitful and was able to forget his past pain and sorrow and forgive his brothers because of God's love. Joseph in Genesis 45:5 says, "But now, do not, therefore, be grieved or angry with yourselves because you sold me here; for God sent me before you to preserve life." Joseph repeats this in verse 8: "So now it was not you who sent me here, but God..." Here is an excellent passage that demonstrates God's sovereignty.

My first grandchild, Cecilia, was born in February 1997. This event enabled me to focus on a new life of joy and blessings. The birth helped me center my thoughts on the future and not on the past. I no longer felt sadness and loneliness every February and March around the anniversary of the death of my sons and my husband. During one of these anniversaries, I received the prayer of deliverance from my pastor, which was a significant part of my healing. I could see the impact of prayer on my children. Our sovereign, loving God inspired these events with His mercy and grace.

There was more healing with each new grandchild. God gave me more blessings: He made me fruitful. My second grandchild was a girl named Teresa. She was born less than two years after my first grandchild. She became my "Angel Teresa," the girl twin I had prayed for before going to visit my sister Cheryl. My son Jack's first child and my first grandson, Malachi, came five years later. Soon after, my daughter Pamela had a son and named him Kevin Matthew after her brother Kevin Michael. My youngest grandchild,

Kaitlyn, was an answer to her brother Malachi's prayer (and mine) for a little sister. There were different aspects of healing for each one of us. God was in control with His love, blessings, and healing power.

Healing came with the passage of time. Time lessened the visceral pain, helped provide perspective, and gave a glimpse of what God could do in and through tragedy. Most of all, healing came with the Holy Spirit's special gift of tongues and my spiritual growth that allowed me to see my life in the sovereignty of God. Time, however, did not remove all pain; it only lessened the pain through the abundant grace of God and the workings of the Holy Spirit.

Lessons Learned

Healing can also come from sharing your hurt and suffering with others. We are most fruitful when we serve others. I worked at a crisis pregnancy center for a short time and was able to share the story of the early deaths of my sons. My goal was to help each mother see the value and worth of her child—to see the baby as a great gift. I did this when discussing the client's personal needs. We all go through the storms of life, but we can come through them and afterward bask in the sunshine of blessings through the grace of God. These clients were also objects of my private intercessory prayer time.

I volunteered with the Big Sisters and Big Brothers organization, which also proved to be an instrument of healing in my life. God used these children to bless me as He used me to bless them. Our God always allows love to flow through us to others and that same virtue to flow back to us.

Before Kevin and Tave passed away, I sponsored children through World Vision because I have always had a great love for children. After their deaths, this devotion was transformed into a mission that provided a source of healing and blessing. The number of children I sponsored increased. These children were in difficult circumstances. They needed the basics—clothes, food, and clean drinking water. One of the World Vision children I sponsored reminded me of Tave. That was an example of our God's love and providence.

Caring for my patients was an opportunity for the comfort and love I received from God to flow through me to them. They were already objects of my intercessory prayers.

God will use every trial, tragedy, hurt, pain, or disappointment in our lives for His glory. He will use us to comfort all those in need with the support we have received from Him, as long as we allow Him to do so. In 2 Corinthians 1:4, Paul says, "... who comforts us in all our tribulation, which we may be able to comfort those who are in any trouble, with the comfort with which we are comforted by God." God sustains us in our tragedies and tribulations, and we can comfort others with the consolation God has given us.

God's Presence is Peace

Our preeminent God not only offers comfort but also calms us and gives us peace. In Luke 8:22–25, Luke tells us Jesus got into a boat with His disciples. Jesus said to them,

> "Let us cross over to the other side of the lake"... But as they sailed He fell asleep. And a windstorm came down on the lake, and they were filling with water and were in jeopardy. And they came to Him and awoke Him, saying, "Master, Master, we are perishing!" Then He arose and rebuked the wind and the raging of the water. And they ceased, and there was calm. But He said to them, "Where is your faith?" And they were afraid, and marveled, saying to one another, "Who can this be? For He commands even the winds and water, and they obey Him!"

When Jesus got into the boat, He said, "Let us go to the other side." Jesus is the word, and the word is truth. Jesus later asked, "Where is your faith?" As we know God more fully, our faith will grow more and more. We can walk through our trials and tragedies, holding onto the hand of our preeminent God, who is love. Exodus 33 tells us how Moses needed the presence of God to get through a difficult time as he led the people of Israel. God allows His glory to shine on us as we cross over our Jordan to the other side with increased faith, blessings, joy, and a realization that we have seen the glory of God as Moses did.

This was my family's and my faith walk to healing. Healing is a lifetime process of drawing closer to the Holy Spirit and Jesus Christ and becoming increasingly like Him. Our spirits will yearn to stand in the gap and intercede for others because of love. In the Lord's Prayer, we ask God that "Thy kingdom come, thy will be done on earth as it is in heaven." Our work is to see God's kingdom on earth and His glory cover the earth as the waters cover the sea. We will be love as Jesus the Christ is love.

A New Ministry

My spiritual response is to comfort others with the comfort I received from God. I send the poem "A Child of Mine," by Edgar Guest, along with scriptures and sayings that I received at the time of my husband's death, to mothers who experience an untimely death of a child. This was not a planned ministry. In fact, I did not see it as a ministry at first. I thought it was the working of the Holy Spirit, the result of the early deaths of my sons. Anytime I heard or read about these incidents in the news, I mailed these two items and shared my testimony. I would also begin praying for them as the Holy Spirit prompted me.

There were times I only knew the child's name, city, and state. I would mail the items and trust God that the mothers would receive them. Many times, I found that they did. I always included my return address, and there were times when the letter was returned to me. When that happened, I would intercede for the parents, trusting God's sovereign and loving care. If I were able to get a complete address later, I'd try again. The first two mothers to whom I mailed these items had lost their children in the daycare center during the Oklahoma City bombing in April 1995. I received a thank-you card from one of the mothers. However, whether or not I receive a response, I trust God and intercede for the parents. I *know* prayer makes a difference. I have been doing this for about twenty years as directed by the Holy Spirit. His love and comfort flow through us to those around us. We are a reflection of His love and Glory.

A Child of Mine
By Edgar Guest

I will lend you, for a little time,
A child of mine, He said.
For you to love the while he lives,
And mourn for when he's dead.
It may be six or seven years,
Or twenty-two or three.
But will you, till I call him back,
Take care of him for Me?
He'll bring his charms to gladden you,
And should his stay be brief,
You'll have his lovely memories,
As solace for your grief.
I cannot promise he will stay,
Since all from earth return.
But there are lessons taught down there,
I want this child to learn.
I've looked the wide world over,
In search for teachers true
And from the throngs that crowd life's lanes,
I have selected you.
Now will you give him all your love,
Nor think the labor vain.

Nor hate me when I come
To take him home again?
I fancied that I heard them say,
"Dear Lord, Thy will be done!"
For all the joys Thy child shall bring,
The risk of grief we'll run.
We'll shelter him with tenderness,
We'll love him while we may,
And for the happiness we've known,
Forever grateful stay.
But should the angels call for him,
Much sooner than we've planned,
We'll brave the bitter grief that comes
And try to understand.

More Reasons to Praise God

Pam, Jack, my husband, and I all had feelings of depression, pain, and loneliness. We shared our feelings and reflections with each other in regards to the death of my boys and God's providence in our lives as a result of everything we had experienced. One step of the grief process is survivor guilt, but God did not allow me to have even one moment of guilt.

After the accident, I did not ask questions about how it had occurred. My husband said that the accident report indicated I might have been distracted by the children in the front seat. I also remember Pamela after the accident saying, "Mama, you stopped." These two facts were only in my subconscious mind. Other than that, I don't recall any of my family over the years saying anything about how the accident happened. I never asked anyone. I know this was God's sovereign work of love and protection. I asked a close friend if I'd ever talked about how the accident might have taken place. She told me that I did share that with her. I know it is possible that over the years I might have heard something about how the accident occurred, but no matter how hard I try, I can't remember. I know that this is due to the love, grace, and protection of our sovereign God as well as that of my family. I'm very thankful for their protective love.

When I started this writing project, my great nephew contributed to the process by doing some research. He decided to get information about the car crash and obtained a copy of the thirty-four-year-old accident report from the local paper. He was born after the crash occurred. He was not aware that I had never seen the article. We were devastated to learn that the article said that I did not stop. That article might explain why so many people were reluctant to talk to me about the accident. Although it was difficult, God had prepared me for that moment by giving me an eyewitness to the accident in the form of my daughter. I believe that God used her to speak the words, "Mama, you stopped."

I understood God's protection even more when I asked Pamela if she saw the article or was aware of it. She said, "I never saw this article." She was not aware of it, but in His sovereign love and protective care of me, God used Pamela many times by letting her say, "Mama, you stopped." I don't understand it all, but I do know that God is awesome. This was only a newspaper article, and God only knows what happened.

I was like David in I Samuel 30:6 after his and his men's wives and children were captured. His men in their grief spoke of stoning David. David remembered all that God had done in the past and inquired of Him in faith and trust. In the same way, I remembered my preeminent God's love and faithfulness over the past thirty-four years and placed my trust and faith in Him. As David did, I decided to commune with God in worship and receive direction.

God did not allow one moment of guilt or questions even after seeing this article. I was filled with trust for our sovereign God. I was filled with praise and awesome wonder of God's care and protection. I was thankful for my parents, brothers, sisters, and husband, who surrounded me with love and protection. The love and grace of our God flowed through them. This was an example of my mother's values of family love and unity that she passed on to us.

I praise God for the spiritual cocoon of love, mercy, and grace that He wrapped around me. The prophet Isaiah says, "When you pass through the waters, I will be with you; and through the rivers, they shall not overflow you. When you walk through the fire, you shall not be burned, Nor shall the flames scorch you" (Isaiah 43:2).

Paul, after the longest extended theological argument in the New Testament (Romans 1:16–11:33), reflects on the incredible wisdom and knowledge of God's in His plan of salvation: "Oh, the depth of the riches both of the wisdom and knowledge of God! How unsearchable are His judgments and His ways past finding out. For who has known the mind of the Lord? Or who has become His Counselor?" (Romans 11:33–34).

It is exciting to marvel at His awesome wisdom and knowledge and to think of the great love, mercy, and grace He lavishes on each one of us. The Psalmist exclaims, "Your mercy, O Lord, is in the heavens; Your faithfulness reaches to the clouds" (Psalm 36:5) and "How precious is Your lovingkindness, O God! Therefore the children of men put their trust under the shadow of Your wings" (Psalm 36:7)

Death of a Child

The death of a child can bring us closer to God and heaven, or it can leave us angry at God. It can cause us to blame God and to run away from Him. This is true with the death of any loved one, but even more so with a child. There are so many questions that cannot and will not be answered on this side of heaven. Our part is to trust God's love and mercy. If we look carefully, we will see His awesome, loving, sovereign character in every happening that surrounds us. Let us not just look at our situation but look at God's face as well. If we solely look at our circumstances, we will misjudge the truth of God's preeminence, power, purpose, and love in the events surrounding us.

The Lord Jesus has gone to prepare a place for those who are His own and tells us, "In my Father's house are many mansions; if it were not so, I would have told you. I go to prepare a place for you. And if I go and prepare a place for you, I will come again and receive you to Myself; that where I am, there you may be also" (John 14:2–3). I don't think that part of this preparation is the death of a child, but knowing your child is with Jesus should make heaven more real and special to you. A child is a precious treasure in heaven. As Jesus says in Matthew 19:14, "Let the little children come to me, and do not forbid them; for of such is the kingdom of heaven." John, in Revelation 21:4, gives us a picture of this heaven when he says, "And God will wipe away every tear from their eyes; there shall be no more death, nor sorrow, nor crying. There shall be no more pain, for the former things have passed away."

Even if the span of your child's life was brief, as my children's were, each child will perform his or her God-given task and will have served a purpose in this world. Your child's presence will have brought out your love, strength, and protection because of his or her helplessness. Your child also will have brought out tenderness and love in you. Your child may have accomplished this in the lives of others as well. A brief life is not always an incomplete life. God is preeminent, and He is love, mercy, and grace.

My almost three-year-old son Tave pointed out Jesus to me many times. Just minutes before his death, he pointed out Jesus the Christ. In Romans 8:28, Paul writes, "And we know that all things work together for good to those who love God, to those who are the called according to His purpose." We don't know how and we don't why. God is sovereign. In some way and somehow, God will make the death of a child or any trial work out for His glory as well as for your good.

God is a God of comfort. He shares our humanity and has compassion for our infirmity. Jesus weeps with us as He wept for Lazarus. St. John records the words, "Jesus wept" (John 11:35). Jesus went to the tomb of Lazarus to restore his life, but He wept. Jesus understands, and He is there to comfort and hold us in His loving arms.

In Luke 7:12–15, we read:

> And when He came near the gate of the city, behold, a dead man was being carried out, the only son of his mother; and she was a widow. And a large crowd from the city was with her. When the Lord saw her, He had compassion on her and said to her, "Do not weep." Then He came and touched the open coffin, and those who carried it stood still. And He said, "Young man, I say to you, arise." So he who was dead sat up and began to speak. And He presented him to his mother.

The Great Shepherd of the sheep, the Lord Jesus Christ, has bent over and reached into His flock and picked up my two lambs, Kevin and Tave, and placed them tenderly under His arms. He is my Savior and friend. He did not do this to rob me, but to lead me upward and higher to greener pastures. He leads me to a more intimate relationship with Him. He is our sovereign God who is Love.

The Sovereignty of God and his Love

LOVE TILL THE LAST NUMBER

Carroll frequently told Pamela, "I love you till the last number."

Whenever she would ask him what the last number was, he responded, "There is no last number." He had that same type of love for his sons as well, but he voiced his love for his daughter more often. Carroll's love for Pamela was a dim reflection of the love our Heavenly Father has for us. My daughter frequently would reflect on what the last number represented. Pamela would understand this more fully as her education progressed. Infinity is expressed mathematically, but it is explained in the teachings and insight of the Holy Spirit.

The Bible tells us in John 3:16, "For God so loved the world that He gave His only begotten Son, that whoever believes in Him should not perish, but have everlasting life." The Bible gives this simple declaration of God's unsurpassed love for us. The Crucifixion demonstrates the depth and tremendous cost of His love.

In Luke 22:42, Jesus says, "Father, if it is Your will, take this cup away from me; nevertheless not my will, but yours, be done." And in verse 44, Luke tells us about Jesus, "And being in agony, He prayed more earnestly. Then His sweat became like great drops of blood falling down to the ground."

In Isaiah 50:6, we read Isaiah's prophecy about Jesus: "I gave My back to those who struck Me, and My cheeks to those who plucked out the beard; I did not hide My face from shame and spitting." The four gospels give us a more detailed picture of the Crucifixion. In Matthew 27:28–31, we are told: "And they stripped Him and put a scarlet robe on Him. When they had twisted a crown of thorns, they put it on His head, and a reed in His right hand. And they bowed the knee before Him and mocked Him, saying 'Hail King of the Jews!' Then they spat on Him and took the reed and struck Him on the head. And when they had mocked Him, they took the robe off Him, put his own clothes on him, and led Him away to be crucified."

Isaiah 53:7 says, "He was oppressed, and He was afflicted, yet He opened not His mouth; He was led as a lamb to the slaughter, and as a sheep before its shearers is silent, so He opened not His mouth." Jesus suffered through humiliation, mocking, was spat on and slapped, yet He was silent. He did not open His mouth.

On the cross, some of His last words were, "Father, forgive them for they know not what they do." Jesus did not sin. He covered Himself with our sins. The scriptures above describing Jesus's words during the Crucifixion give us a broader picture of the father's love. What it cost God the father to send His only son to suffer and die such a horrific death on the cross cannot be grasped entirely through the reading of these scriptures. I know that with the power of intercession, the Holy Spirit can enlighten us and open our eyes so that we begin to grasp the depth of God's love. Intercession is a prayer that pleads with God for the needs of others. But it is also much more than that. Intercession involves taking hold of God's will and refusing to let go until it comes to pass.

Isaiah 55:8–9 tells us, "'For My thoughts are not your thoughts, nor are your ways My ways,' says the Lord. 'For as the heavens are higher than the earth, so are My ways higher than your ways, and My thoughts than your thoughts.'" No one but the Holy Spirit, who comes from the father, can reveal the unfathomable depths of His sovereignty and love.

God is preeminent as Isaiah tells us in 45:18: "For thus says the Lord, Who created the heavens, Who is God, Who formed the earth and made it, Who has established it, Who did not create it in vain, Who formed it to be inhabited: 'I am the Lord, and there is no other.'"

Love

Love is a choice. I Corinthians 13:4–7 says, "Love suffers long and is kind; love does not envy; love does not parade itself, is not puffed up; does not behave rudely, does not seek its own, is not provoked, thinks no evil; does not rejoice in iniquity, but rejoices in the truth; bears all things, believes all things, hopes all things, endures all things."

Love is not some of these aspects; it is all of these together. I Corinthians 13:8 says, in part, that love never fails. All of these elements point to the power of love, which speaks of character more than feelings. Love is a choice we make as we relate to each other every day. Love is also a choice we make when we respond to life's challenges. Being patient and kind are some of the ways of being that create the feelings we all ascribe to the word *love*.

God is love. The story of redemption in the Bible, from Genesis to Revelation, is possible only because of our God's love for His created world. In spite of the world's fallen state, God's grace and love were able to intervene in it through His son and do things exceedingly and abundantly and beyond anything we could imagine. Without the sovereign love of the father mediated through Jesus Christ the son and confirmed through the Holy Spirit, there would be no freedom from sin and death and no hope of everlasting life.

Sovereignty of God

The sovereignty of God refers to His unlimited power and control over nature and history. He is under no rule or authority outside Himself. God is omniscient and has superior knowledge and wisdom.

Job 42:2 says, "I know that You can do everything And that no purpose of Yours can be withheld from You." Psalm 86:10 says, "For You are great, and do wondrous things; You alone are God. God knows our thoughts and ways." Isaiah 40:13–14 says: "Who has directed the Spirit of the Lord, Or as His counselor has taught Him? With whom did He take counsel, and who instructed Him, And taught Him in the path of justice? Who taught Him knowledge, And showed Him the way of understanding?"

Our God is omniscient. He is in all places and every situation at once. Hebrews 1:3 says, "Who being the brightness of His glory and the express image of His person, and upholding all things by the word of His power, when He had by Himself purged our sins, sat down at the right hand of the Majesty on high."

Our sovereign God is omnipresent. Psalm 139:7–12 asks,

> Where can I go from Your Spirit?
> Or where can I flee from Your presence?
> If I ascend into heaven, You are there;
> If I make my bed in hell, behold, You are there.
> If I take the wings of the morning,
> And dwell in the uttermost parts of the sea,
> Even there your hand shall lead me,
> And your right hand shall hold me.
> If I say, "Surely the darkness shall fall on me,"
> Even the night shall be light about me;
> Indeed, the darkness shall not hide from You,
> But the night shines as the day;
> The darkness and the light are both alike to You.

In the context of my journey, this psalm speaks of God's presence through the trials of my life. Whether I've been in a dark and deep valley or have felt His boundless grace and mercy manifested in strength, joy, and peace, He is always with me.

Our sovereign God who is love sent His only son to suffer and die on the cross for our sins. In the book 1 John 3:1 are the words: "Behold what manner of love the Father has bestowed on us, that we should be called children of God!" This love was through Jesus coming to earth and living among us. God then sent the Holy Spirit to us on the day of Pentecost (Acts 2). Paul tells us in 1 Corinthians 2:12, "Now we have received, not the spirit of the world, but the Spirit who is from God, that we might know the things that have been freely given to us by God."

Mercy

Mercy is compassion or forgiveness shown toward someone whom it is within one's power to punish or harm for some wrong or sin committed. Our pride often causes us to overlook this aspect of mercy. Our sovereign, loving God is a God of mercy. Immediately after the fall of man, God talked about the disease of human sin and specified the cure for it. He did not give us what we deserved. God gave us mercy and placed our sins on His only son, Jesus Christ. He took us under His wings of love. In Genesis 13, He says to the serpent:

> And I will put enmity
> Between you and the woman,
> And between your seed and her seed;
> He shall bruise your head,
> And you shall bruise His heel.

The whole redemptive story of the Bible is the fulfillment of that prophecy by our sovereign God, as Paul teaches in Romans 8–11.

Grace

Grace is the undeserving favor of God to those who are under condemnation. God's grace is the salvation of sinners and the blessings. John 1:14–16 states, "And the Word became flesh and dwelt among us, and we beheld His glory, the glory as of the only begotten of the Father, full of grace and truth. And of His fullness, we have all received, and grace for grace." The fact that grace came from His fullness teaches us that grace is more than God's disposition or impersonal favor; it is God meeting us at our point of need in the person of Jesus Christ. Isaiah 53:6 tells us we are all like sheep, we have gone astray, and we wander. The finding and saving are all in the hands of Jesus Christ. Jesus, the lamb of God, the perfect sacrifice, took our sins on Himself. That was grace for us. God demonstrates His power, wisdom, love, and even miracles when we place our faith and trust in Jesus Christ.

The Holy Spirit will empower us to bring God's kingdom on earth as it is in heaven. Paul, in Romans 14:17, says, "… for the Kingdom of God is not eating and drinking, but righteousness and peace and joy in the Holy Spirit." This same Spirit that raised Jesus from the dead dwells within each one of us and teaches us all things. The Spirit teaches us the word. Jesus is the word.

Psalm 119:89 tells us, "Forever, O Lord, Your Word is settled in Heaven." Jesus, in Matthew 24:35, says, "Heaven and earth will pass away, but My Words will by no means pass away."

Today

The working of the Holy Spirit and my sovereign God of mercy, grace and love has brought my surviving children and me to a place a place of restoration and growth in Christ. God has used our trials, tests, and tragedies to mold us closer to the image of Christ. The Holy Spirit has enabled us to see the world through the eyes of Jesus. We have learned not to hold on too tightly to the things of this world but to use them for God's glory and kingdom. We understand the brevity of life. Life is to be spent in loving and sharing the gospel of Jesus with our brothers and sisters on earth as one family in Christ. My children are passing these truths to their children, and it is my hope that in ten generations, these truths will be passed on to children yet to be born.

Pamela's father would always say that he loved her "till the last number," and we have learned that God's love stretches into infinity. His Love is abundant, and we desire that it flow from us to those around us.

Pamela and her husband, John, live in La Serena, Chile. John works for the Gemini Observatory. Both have doctorates from the Massachusetts Institute of Technology. Pamela now understands her father's words, "I love you till the last number." They have three children: Cecilia (twenty-two), Teresa (twenty-one), and Kevin (fourteen) whom Pamela homeschools.

Carroll Jack and his wife, Trinia, live in Seattle, Washington, where they are active in their local church and participate in local ministry opportunities. Jack is a project manager, and Trinia is a homemaker and a literacy tutor. They have two children, Malachi (sixteen) and Kaitlyn (eleven).

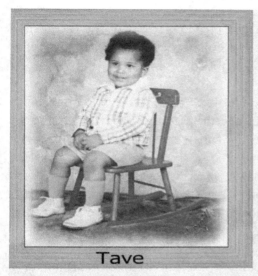

Tave

Tave & Mom

Tave

Kevin
(in gymnastics uniform)

Kevin & Tave

Kevin

97

About the Author

Geraldine D. Washington is a retired registered nurse. After she received her BS in Nursing in 1967, she worked in pediatrics, surgery, medicine, and obstetrics and for many years as a night supervisor.

She worked as the head nurse of a detoxification (detox) unit that helped patients recover from alcohol and drug abuse. During that time, she spent many hours at home, praying for her patients in their battle against substance abuse.

After retirement in 2001, she worked at a pregnancy center and clinic as a nurse and volunteer, saving mothers and babies from abortion. She also prayed privately for each client's problem.

She received a doctorate in theology from Christian Life School of Theology on October 10, 2007. Today, she is active in her church's ministries. Her focus is intercessory prayer, homeless feeding programs, and Bible study. She spends part of her time visiting those confined to nursing homes, praying with them and offering friendship. She spends much of her time as an intercessor for our nation, its leaders, her church, friends, and family.

She enjoys reading and visiting her children and grandchildren in the Pacific Northwest and Canada.